UNSILENCED

FACES OF DOMESTIC VIOLENCE SURVIVAL

Presented By

LA'TICIA NICOLE

Published by: Purposely Created Publishing Group™
Printed in the United States of America

ISBN-10: 1-942-83817-4
ISBN-13: 978-1-942838-17-3

Table of Contents

Introduction

According to the National Domestic Violence Hotline, in the United States alone, 24 people per minute become victims of rape, physical violence, or stalking by an intimate partner. Over the course of a year, that equals over 12 million people. Notice that I said *people* instead of women. Although the number of affected women far exceeds that of men, the fact still stands that domestic violence can happen to anyone, regardless of your gender, place of birth, age, race, sexual orientation, tax bracket, education level, etc. It's the third leading cause of homelessness, and one out of every three female homicide victims are murdered by either their current or former romantic partner.

Those fortunate enough not to have been victims of domestic violence oftentimes believe that it couldn't happen to them because they know better or they wouldn't play that, but that's simply not true. I was actually that woman once upon a time. I considered myself a pretty strong person. Prior to becoming *that woman*, I would tell you exactly what I'd do and how I'd handle it if a man were to put his hands on me. I was being judgmental. When it actually happened to me, in retrospect, I felt like God allowed it to happen so that He could trust me to use sympathy and empathy when I speak to domestic violence.

And because I had not actually been involved in domestic violence to that extent, as a motivational speaker, I couldn't speak to that particular situation because I couldn't understand why women would stay, and, if they were mothers, why they would continuously put their children through some mess like that. I didn't realize that when you're a victim of domestic violence, you're not in your right state of mind. That's why I decided to create this anthology. For someone to hear or read my story is one thing, but to read a collection of testimonies is another. That's what this is—a gathering of eight women, sharing their most personal and vulnerable experiences in hopes of the strong woman, the smart woman, and even the woman who seemingly has it all together will pick up this book and gain something from these chapters that will further encourage her as a woman, mother, friend, sister, aunt, cousin, co-worker, and neighbor.

Let's use our voices, resources and advice to empower abused and battered women who are seeking spiritual guidance on how to develop the courage to safely escape their abusers and restore their hope and confidence.

The Escape

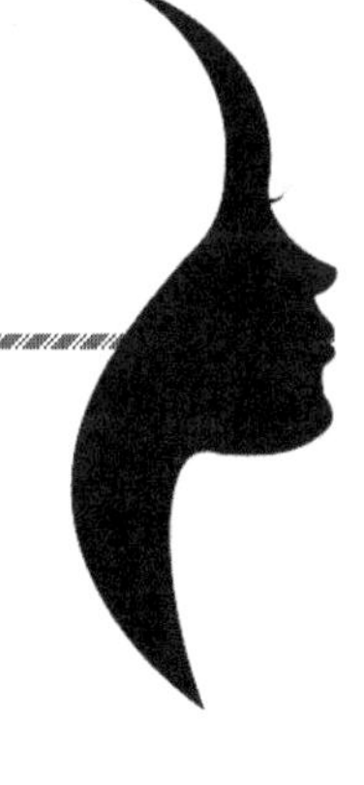

Standing still as down fall the rain,

Disguising outside visible with pain,

Unveiled face withdrawn from fallen tears,

Cloudy waters hiding all apparent fears,

It's just little things deep inside of me,

Dreaming of what the mind begins to see,

There's nothing in this world I'd rather do,

Than allow thunderstorms to erase outlined images of you.

Slowly lowering eyes to wetness beneath my feet,

Gazes of reflection to focused expression meet,

Wondering how she escaped from instilled scars,

Sleeping soundly in the comfort of unmarked cars,

While raising her head to stars above,

Softly speaking, "Lord, send me peace significant to a pure white dove."

All as a woman, my heart won't let it be,

In life with strength I need to be set free!

- Spicee Gray

1

I Am Favored

LA'TICIA NICOLE

I stood in the mirror, staring at myself, looking for something, anything, worthy of being confident in and proud of. My eyes were both swollen and blackened, and, as the old saying goes, I was sick and tired of being sick and tired. For the life of me, I couldn't figure out how I ended up wearing the shoes of a battered woman. Then again, did that label apply to me? After all, we fought. He hit me, and I hit back. In the backseat of a taxi, just hours before, we went at it.

I was still married at the time. Legally separated, but married still. My emotions were out of whack, and my confidence was shot. I guess you can say I was an open target because I was hurt and confused and kept attracting the same soul with a different face. It's like the devil knows exactly what you like and want and won't hesitate to bait you with it—just the way you like it. This one was a businessman. He was handsome, smelled nice, real savvy, and wore bow ties. As a matter of fact, it was the bow tie that popped it all off.

My side hustle consisted of selling accessories. He'd purchased a bow tie from me and later wore it to impress me. He made it known from the jump that he was interested in me, but I let him chase me for a little while before agreeing to let him take me out. I learned that we were (allegedly) in the same predicament: married, but separated. So I didn't see a problem with it, and the more we went out, the more emotionally invested I became. He appeared to be everything that I wanted and needed, so I was happy. I thought that I'd finally met my match, my one.

I met his family and everything. He treated me to breakfast, lunch, and dinner, and since my kids were with their father on the weekends, he'd spend Saturdays and Sundays at my place. Did we ever spend time over at his house? No. Did I find that suspicious? Yes. His reasoning was that his wife was still in the process of moving out, so she and the kids were still coming and going. Out of respect, he preferred that we wait until the ordeal was over and done with. Made sense to me and because my divorce wasn't yet finalized, I had a little patience and understanding to spare.

Also, considering the amount of time we spent together, it was practically impossible for him and his wife not to have been separated. In addition to my house being his weekend getaway, we'd roam the town together (which wasn't all that big, by the way) and take frequent vacations. For my birthday that year, for instance, we went to Miami together. Ordinarily, I'd take a trip with a group of girlfriends, but because so many didn't agree with my relationship with him, that left me with only one who was still willing to go.

During this trip, I realized just how *deep* his bad habits were. One, he was extremely jealous. Although it was annoying, initially, I kind of saw his possessiveness as him wanting me. In that sense, it made me feel prized and valuable. Being jealous of me dancing or having a good time with someone else, I can almost understand. But turning green-faced because someone else was merely looking at me was a bit much. On several instances during the trip, my friend would call him out on his ridiculousness.

"See, this is what I'm talking about," he said as we were walking down the strip on Ocean Drive. He was losing his mind, fussing, cussing, and trying to fight everybody who looked at me too long. Never mind if someone had said something to me! As if any of his behavior was logical, he kept turning to my friend to back him up. Then she got fed up and asked him, "What do you want me to do? Put a bag over her head? She's pretty, they're going to look." It was like he didn't even hear her; his jealousy didn't allow him to comprehend rationale.

On top of being jealous, he had a terrible drinking problem. He was the type of drunk who was reckless, violent, and spoke the straight truth when intoxicated. One day while riding in the car together, he slurred about how me and his wife didn't deserve him. Mind you, they were supposedly separated. Because he never remembered the things he said or did while drunk, I asked him if I could record him. He agreed to it, so I pulled out my cellphone and recorded his whole ranting session.

"She's Hillary Clinton and you're ride or die, and neither of you are going anywhere," he said. "Your husband is an old washer and dryer ass nigga. We're Versace and he's South Pole."

The next morning, I replayed it so he could hear how crazy he sounded. Instead of acknowledging his drunk actions and confessions, he was upset about me recording him, asking why I did it without permission. That experience let me know who I was dealing with. He would never admit that he was wrong unless I was about to walk out of the door, and even then, it wouldn't be sincere. By nature, I'm not only forgiving, but I'm also optimistic and persistent, so I stuck around.

On that same trip to Miami, he tested me once more by going so far (or should I say so low) as to try to hook up with my best friend. I was intoxicated and had passed out in my friend's lap. I recall hearing the two of them talking, but can't recall exactly what they were saying. I do remember waking up with the dire need to pray and crawling into a corner. I laid there in a fetal position, holding myself. I went from rocking to praying to speaking in tongues and shouting. Right there in the middle of my mess, the Holy Spirit had washed over me.

My friend would later tell me that not only did he try to come on to her, but he'd stated that he was in training to become ordained. That he wanted me to be his first lady, but worried that I may not have been cut out for the job. Not long after that, I'd gotten up to pray in the corner. She told him then that it's not me we needed to be worried about; it was him. That brings me to my first point of dealing with domestic violence. It may not be you who's dealing with it, but someone who you know. Although your loved one may not take your advice or disclose the truth with you, it's important to be there for them. I thank God for my friend being in my corner because I was genuinely confused.

I'd go to church and he'd be in the parking lot, drinking and waiting for me to get out. He'd send angry texts asking how long I was going to be in there, telling me to hurry up and calling me a liar because I'd said that service was only an hour. Although he was getting on my last nerve and I had every reason to get out of that relationship, I held on. Like I said, I was confused. I was vulnerable, emotionally unstable, and suffering from a severe case of low self-esteem. On top of that, shame was involved. I was already one foot off of my marriage, so another failed relationship, in my opinion, would have confirmed that the problem was me.

On one hand, I knew that I needed to get away from him. Not only was he abusive, but he was still dealing with his wife. They weren't even separated. Every piece of evidence that I needed, I got. One occasion, he pocket dialed me, and I heard the entire conversation between him and his wife, and it sounded like a happy home. On another, I read the text messages and got the same happy-home picture. Then there was the time he lied about meeting his wife to discuss the divorce. He claimed that he needed to see how much she'd need considering she had the kids and everything. The next thing I knew, one of my girlfriends, who lived in his neighborhood, called me and said that he and his wife were walking down the street exercising and laughing. When I confronted him about it, he said that they didn't want to talk about it in front of the kids, so they went for a walk to do it. Once again, I believed him.

On the other hand, leaving was difficult. As hard as he would fight when angry or drunk is how hard he would fight to keep the relationship going. He'd promise me the world and everything in it. He'd promise that he wouldn't do it again. He even had his mama lying for him. It took close to a year of all that drama and abuse and heartbreak after heartbreak for me to finally throw my hands in the air and cut it off. It happened during a trip to Maryland. We'd gone to a club one night and a waitress stopped to dance with me. He got jealous of her and we started arguing. He ended up hitting me in the face twice. My forehead protruded, and my eyes were black. I started throwing bottles, cracked him in the face, and he started bleeding. I got put out.

I was so disoriented that I didn't know where I was or how to get back to the hotel. I caught a cab alone with a strange man, trying to find a hotel that I neither knew the name or address of with no money or anything. That was it for me. When I finally did make it back to the right hotel, security escorted me to our room to get my stuff, and he was there asleep. I walked up to him and punched him in the face then left. Fortunately, the hotel gave me a room that night in spite of me not being able to pay for it.

That was my breaking point because anything could've happened to me that night. I stood in the mirror of my hotel room staring at my blackened eyes and busted lip. I started realizing what had happened. Because I was so empty inside, I needed desperately to fill that void. That's what he was for me: a filling. However, he was doing far more harm than good. And even if he did leave his wife, I neither wanted nor needed him in my life anymore. He could've *killed* me and taken me from my children. In that moment, I knew that I had two choices: I could keep searching for love and ending up in this same predicament, or I could start working on loving me and getting to know who I was and what I wanted. I chose the latter.

Before entering a relationship, make sure that you're not doing it to make anyone else happy. If you're not happy with yourself, don't do it. Be whole *before* you enter a relationship because two halves don't equal a whole, believe it or not. If you're already in an abusive relationship, know that you deserve better. You don't have to settle. Someone out there is looking for you, but he can't find you because you're settling for this mess. If your mother didn't name you that, don't allow him, or anyone else, to call you out of your name. Furthermore, don't allow anyone to label you, even if it's something as seemingly innocent and cute as "spoiled," because that's how it starts. It starts with a word. "You're ugly; you're fat; you're stupid."

Understand that when you're being abused, you're not in your right mind. You're not in contentment with who you are. You're trying to find something and fill a void. I was able to feel that when this man came into my life saying I needed some vitamin K, some sunshine. I like trips, shopping, and being taken care of, so the devil knew exactly the type of person to bring into my life. But it was a trick and that's how I got into that. Consider what traps can be used against you.

And if you aren't being abused, but may know someone who is, signs to look out for include him talking down to her and not allowing her to go somewhere as if she's a child. She has to ask to buy a pair of shoes or get her hair done even though she works 40 hours a week, and she doesn't come around like she used to. You better believe that there's something going on there. Don't just leave her out there because she has someone. It might not be because she's happy. That's not normal behavior, especially if you all used to hang out regularly before she got involved with him. She may be at home with a busted lip, scared to talk to anybody. Check on your friend, and if she denies it, then just continue to be there for her. Be that listening ear.

Communicate effectively, being careful not to scare her away. You want her to feel as though she has someone to talk to, so don't continuously talk about the man. Otherwise, she won't be able to be around you—she'll feel as though you're judging her. It's a fine line because it's hard; we don't want to see our friend hurt, but we also don't want to push them away. Keep an open line of communication, so that she'll know that you're there and that she can always come to you to talk or for help—whether it's a midnight phone call to cry or request to be picked up.

Anyone can be affected by domestic violence—the strong woman, the street smart woman, the college-educated woman, and the woman who seemingly has it all together and doesn't need a man because her finances are good. Never judge a book by its cover since you never know what a woman is using to hide herself because we are quick to hide ourselves beneath Bobbi Brown, Mac, and Fashion Fair, but God knows when we're not happy for real. That's what was revealed to me. It's like my mask was taken off. No longer could I use makeup to cover up my bruises. It was one thing when I was able to put Mac on my face to paint on my smile, but I couldn't cover those marks and bruises up with powder.

We should never think that we would never go through it because it's possible. And you never know who's going through it, so pay attention. Domestic violence—be it verbal, physical, sexual, emotional, etc.—is equally detrimental and correlated. However, we're a force to be reckoned with when we unite.

Together, we can *#SpeakLife* to finally end domestic violence in our homes, families and communities.

Repeat After Me:

> I AM blessed.
> I AM valued.
> I AM healthy.
> I AM rich.

I bind strife, confusion, and envy.
I rebuke generational curses.
I release a spirit of peace because I have joy.

I do not have the spirit of fear.

I AM delivered and set free from bondage.

I AM more than a conqueror through Jesus.

I AM a new person.
Old things have passed away.
My past doesn't define me.
I like me.
In fact, I love me.
And I forgive me.

I love the Lord and He loves me.
I have the favor of God on my life.

I *#SpeakLife* into all dead situations.

La' Ticia

2

I Am Worthy

KIMBERLY SESSOMS

Growing up in a loving family as the youngest of three children, life was good for the most part. We had issues and family problems just like everybody else, but my parents took really good care of us. We ate dinner together, took family vacations, and, most importantly, our home was filled with love. My father was an awesome provider while my mom made sure the house was cleaned; that's where I learned to take care of a house and see a man as basically a caregiver. I was a very quiet child, but I paid close attention to what was happening in my home. Yes, there were arguments, and sometimes the fussing was so loud, I just stayed in my room. Being the youngest, I experienced a lot more than my brother and sister.

Through my years growing up, I never had a problem getting a boyfriend. The quiet ones didn't interest me. On the other hand, the ones who only wanted sex, aggravated you, was wanted by everybody else, were my problem. Of course, I chose what many called the "bad boy." He dressed nice and had the hottest car in town. I was the girl who could go out on a weeknight because I had a lot of freedom with my curfew, so I was pretty much always available for him.

Truthfully, I saw many warning signs, but I just knew I had him. When you are dating a guy and he disappears and always is with his boys at strange times...yep, those are warning signs. When you start doing things like sneaking out of the house, you know there is a problem because that person is causing you to be out of your normal character. I can say, when you are in love, or what you think is love, it will make you do crazy things. For example, you find out he's seeing someone else and you know it, but he keeps lying. Because you are still getting his time since the other chick can't go out or have company, you feel content. What would you call that? Desperate or someone who just wants who they want? By this time, we had become intimate, which only adds fuel to the fire because deeper emotions are involved. What's even sadder is when those close to you know the person is no good, but they allow you to stay in the relationship anyway. If you have friends and family giving you sound advice, please take heed.

Fast forward to several break ups due to cheating and lies later. After I moved to Maryland and he went back to New York, we agreed to a long distance relationship. Before I knew it, I was pregnant! We decided to move back to North Carolina and get married before the baby was born. We also took counseling sessions with the pastor who was going to perform the ceremony. Although we had to live with my parents, it was all good in the beginning. We were ecstatic over our baby girl, but it didn't take long for him to start running the streets again with his boys. I took my responsibility seriously, even the marriage, at age 18. Thank God for family support; I have the best parents. He grew up without his father, and his mom wasn't too happy about the marriage or baby. She always treated my daughter differently than her other grandchildren.

We eventually moved out into our own apartment, and it didn't take long for him to get into the game, meaning selling drugs. When he did have a job, he barely went. He'd call in sick using the excuse that someone in his family had died. I'd never in my life met someone who had just about killed off their entire family to avoid going to work. On top of that, he would get paid on Friday, and his entire check would be gone by Saturday. He wouldn't come home until 4 a.m. some nights, and questioning him about his whereabouts would set him off.

I was the kind of wife who got up and cooked him breakfast before work and dinner was ready if and when he decided to come home from work. He was just all about himself. There was an incident when he was locked up, for example, and owed the drug man money. This put our family in jeopardy, but, again, a person who is all about themselves doesn't care if they are putting others' lives in harm's way.

In spite of his selfishness, the evidence of cheating and rumors, I still decided to stay. If someone tells you they saw his car in the alley, believe them. If you see his friend driving his car, know it's not just a coincidence—something is up. Never get mad at yourself for overlooking many signs.

These are the things I learned from my mother who was a great role model.

Next came the hitting, so I had him arrested several times, but I always allowed him to come back. He had an aunt who spoiled him, so she paid all our bills and gave him whatever he wanted, even a motorcycle. Every time I called the police, his family came to his defense and said it wouldn't happen again. One night, he got so upset that he pulled a gun on me while I was in my daughter's room. I knew then I had to leave the situation. My only concern was my daughter's safety.

By that time, we had started going back to church, but nothing changed. If you are ever in a situation like this or similar, don't say it will never happen again—get out. If I had just one dollar for all the times he said he was sorry and it wouldn't happen again, I would be seriously rich. Never allow a man to use the excuse of not having a father growing up for why he acts a certain way. There are plenty of people from broken homes who treat people the right way; these are just excuses. You have to love yourself more than a man who will verbally abuse you or put his hands on you because that isn't love. Talk to your family because that support will help you get through. Never deal with this kind of situation alone. Though I was young, I still wanted my marriage to work, but I finally learned it takes relying on other people. I had my mind made up that I had done all I could, and I didn't want to jeopardize my life any longer.

If you have a place to go, please do so, and don't take up for them. Even in the midst of all this turmoil, I was able to get a job and my associate's degree. If you have goals and dreams, but you are in a relationship or situation that is causing you to give up or feel less than, begin to encourage yourself every day. There are many songs and books we can use to help us motivate ourselves, especially if you don't feel comfortable talking to anyone. Nobody loves us more than God, and He will not let us down. Depression and isolation can bring on crazy thoughts like not wanting to live any longer. Don't let it get to that point. Please seek help. I've been there, and it gets better. You just have to want better for yourself, and then take the necessary steps to make that happen.

Never be too hard on yourself because we all have a breaking point. Sometimes we can love too hard and think we can change a person. Even after the gun incident, some time passed and I gave it one more chance. We made a move to Maryland, and I just knew things would be different. I felt that if I got him away from his current environment, he'd be willing to change. As we all know, if the person doesn't have a made up mind to seek help, things will remain the same, which they did. However, getting hit in my head with brass knuckles was it. I said, "Lord, I need your help to put this man out." I called the police again, and I was done and never looked back. After he moved out, it was just me and my baby girl in Maryland at the time. Imagine how you would feel if you came home and most of your furniture was gone. Well, when in the drug game, people don't care about anybody but themselves. He of course didn't pay a debt, so they came and cleaned out our house. I had my moments of down talking myself, but I didn't stay there. We as abused women can be very hard on ourselves, but know that no matter what, you deserve the best. The best thing about that situation was that it drew me closer to God. Not to say I didn't make more mistakes, but I know there was nothing too hard for my Savior, and He came through every time just when I needed Him the most.

Look back over your life and see how many times God has stepped in and made a way. *My God!* We all have a story, so let mine and yours be a success story to help others along the way. I now know God didn't give this to me just for me. I understand how people get caught up in bad situations because we allow men to make us feel less than worthy of the best or at least that we don't deserve something better. If you are in a situation where you have to hide your wallet, lie about who you talk to, and are afraid to sleep at night, please seek help.

There was something instilled in me at an early age to be a fighter, no matter how many times I got knocked down or didn't seem to want it anymore. Once you have another life you are responsible for, things will change quickly. I had to make things happen. So, with family and working, I kept on going. Even though I spent many nights lying in bed with tears rolling down my face, I kept going because I never wanted my daughter or family to see me that way.

Take heed to any signs, and never believe it will not happen again. Pray and seek God's guidance, seek help from family and friends, and most importantly understand that it's not your fault. If you are a part of a church, there are always women's groups you can join, and your pastor is always a great place to start. I've taken advantage of all these resources, even counseling, because this kind of damage can have a lifelong effect on a person. One major thing I've realized is what's "enough" for me isn't the same for someone else.

Protect yourself in the future by refusing to allow anyone to steal your joy. Ask yourself how they react when things don't go their way. How do they deal with adversary? How was their family life growing up? Sometimes I sit back and wonder why I put up with this behavior and how I allowed myself to be used that way. Truthfully, I really don't know, but I do know that God was my saving grace because no serious harm was ever done to me or my daughter, well physically.

Yes, these things can cause emotional damage, which is why you should seek whatever you need and never let others tell you to just move on and let it go. Emotional feelings like this will come back to haunt you years later and could affect your current relationships because of undealt with issues and feelings. However, thank God for giving you a major testimony that will inspire and encourage someone else. We are more than conquerors, and God is not a man that He should lie. We are His children and He wants the best for us, and I challenge you to tell yourself this and make it a daily affirmation. We are survivors. Know that God can do all things, and there is nothing too hard for Him.

Kim

Black-Out

Stretched with dry waterfalls
lined down her pale face,

Silver metal content laid upon as a temporary place,

Attempting to retract how one landed a cold room:

Visions in head are blurry with outlines of gloom,

Surrounding echo voices speaking from medical terms of technology;

She did not go to college, but one appeared degree of biology,

White covering shield blocking optical sight,

All is not dark for there's a faded gleaming light,

Footsteps are to pavement as temperature never begin to change;

She can't feel a heartbeat for no emotion is in range,

A hand lowers to head removing cloth of protection,

In glass above mounted flat one mirrored reflection,

Eyes positioned towards the ceiling without a minute's blink,

Now being motionless, she won't have to even think,

The face is unrecognizable for any human being to see,

I'm lying lifeless because he took all his anger out on me.

- *Spicee Gray*

I Am a Believer

MARICE BEATTY

There I was, a scared, skinny sophomore in high school, walking down the hall of a healthcare clinic with my mind in such a daze that I did not see my grandparents walking toward me! The nurse's voice echoed in my mind, "Your pregnancy test came back positive." My mother had already called my grandparents and told them she thought I was pregnant and that I was at the clinic. When I looked up and saw the look on my grandfather's face as he walked toward me, I could feel his disappointment, and I just wanted to go somewhere and hide from shame. Thinking about that day brings tears to my eyes. You see, I believe I always carried a special place in my grandfather's heart, and on that day, he was hurt, and I could feel his heartbreak.

As I learned early on in life, this too shall pass. You see, my grandfather's love was greater than that disappointment. He let me know early on that it was not going to be easy, but I was going to finish high school, and he expected me to do great things with my life. Looking back now, I was 15 years old when I initially found out I was going to be a mother for the first time in my life, and I did not know squat about being a mother. Yes, I was smart and I was kind and even knew how to cook a little, but to prepare a life for a baby and myself for day-to-day tasks on a 15-year-old's budget? *Right*...what budget? I was not prepared, but God kept me sane. He surely guided my footsteps, and I had what some do not have today—strong family support!

I started working and making a little money. My grades were good and I even had a car, but when it appears things are going good, there is always a "but." By this time, two years had passed, and I was working part-time on a cafeteria line in a hospital. I was also dating during this time, but nothing too serious because I was in my senior year of high school, and I was just focused on having fun. That is, until I met the man I thought I was going to spend the rest of my life with. Wouldn't you know it, at the end of my senior year, I was pregnant for the second time? I met "baby daddy" when he started working at the hospital with me. When we first met, he remembered me from the neighborhood. After working together for some time, and since he already knew my family, I figured we would be a good fit. Never judge a book by its cover.

We started dating, and it kind of got crazy early on in the relationship. If I could go back, I'd tell myself that if you are arguing to the point that one of you raises your hand at the other... RUN, GO, and don't stop to collect $200. But at that time in my life, I was young, unfocused, and so in love—or so I thought I was. So of course I did not see the warning signs of controlling behavior, isolation from my friends and family, jealousy, and blaming others for his problems, nor did I want to see them. I know that attachment you feel with the one you have laid with, given your heart to, and made a baby with. You just knew he was going to be the one until you began to see his true colors, but again, this too shall pass. Let's take a walk down memory lane with my "baby daddy."

Baby Daddy had a little hood in him. I thought it was all for show, but I learned differently after being pinned up against that wall and choked one night. As I stood there, pinned up against that wall, facing this man with cold, dark eyes, I trembled with tears in my eyes. I had been pushed into a corner, which meant that I needed to fight for my life. I realized that I had my keys in my hand, so without thought, I used those keys as a weapon and dug them into his face until he let me go. Once he released me, I got out of that house like a bat out of hell. I was driving so fast, one would have thought I was in the Indy 500 race. I even got stopped by a policeman right up from his house. Looking back, I do not know why I did not send that policeman to his house or report it then and there, but, like many who have faced domestic violence, I looked at the situation/fight as just an argument that got out of hand. Like I said, sometimes we do not want to see the signs when they are right there.

A few days later, I went right back to Baby Daddy. I remember walking into his mother's house and she told me, "You betta not mess up my baby face anymore." I politely told her, "Well, you need to tell your baby to keep his hands from around my neck then." We have to not allow the enemy to trick us into believing that such behavior is normal. People who truly love each other do not hurt each other or put one another in harm's way. Yes, we go into relationships as individuals, and we are going to have a difference of opinions. Some have little habits that may get under one's skin, but when you truly love one another, you learn to discuss things rationally. You are not aiming to hurt one another because when they hurt, you hurt, even with words.

A few weeks later, Baby Daddy and some friends got into a fight, and there were some consequences that resulted from this fight, leading to a lot of back and forth going downtown to court. I clearly remember the day his mother told him she was not going to court with him, and her "baby" threw the kitchen chair at her! When a man does not honor and respect his mother...RUN! You see, that was another sign I chose not to see at the time. He was blaming others for his trouble, saying such things to his mother like, "You have never been there for me. You never did anything for me..." He was grown and still living at home with his mother washing his clothes and cooking his food and probably paying half his car loan. Here I was, a mother of two children with my own apartment and now working full-time in the cafeteria, having lost my car and was riding the bus or with him.

Often we give and over-protect our youth so much as they are growing up that they grow up not knowing how to earn or manage money. Over-protected children also grow up to be disrespectful to people, and they become lost. For example, he felt that he could tell me when and where I could go and who I could go with. And if I was not home when he called, it was on and popping like popcorn. We had pagers back then instead of cell phones, so I had to be home when he called or return his call within a specific amount of time. I never gave him a key to my place, but I came home at least three times and found him in my apartment. To this day, I *still* do not know how he was getting inside my apartment.

This leads me to the beginning of my isolation. You know when your man keeps telling you he does not want you to hang out with your girls or your family because he wants to be with you? Or, if you invite him along to a family outing, he says no because your family does not like him, so he tries to make you feel guilty about leaving him or the baby? Then, when it's time for him to roll out, he does not think twice about asking you to go anywhere with him. Yeah, that's what I was dealing with.

If I did go somewhere, he was clocking me like I was on his dime. He wanted to know where I was going to be, who was going to be there, what time I was coming home, and I'm pretty sure he was doing a few drive-bys just to make sure. Since he already knew my family, I was sure we were going to be a good fit. *The devil is a liar!* I was in prison. Even though I had my own place, I stayed at the house with him and his mom more than half the time because, in his eyes, I could not wash the baby's clothes correctly or change and feed the baby correctly. Since I was young and in love, I thought he meant well. What he was really doing, however, was degrading me and decreasing my self-esteem every minute.

One weekend, I wanted to hang out with my friends and family. I went home, and he was in my apartment, waiting for me when I opened the door. We started fighting right as we walked in. I say "we" because my girlfriends, Ragan and Lacy, were not going to allow him to place his hands on me. Now this is when the MC Hammer pants and shoes were out, so I thought I was cute until I slid across that floor—not dancing, but from him hitting me. I was confused. We tore my stairs up that day, but when he left, we both looked like we had been in a fight. All because I was out having fun with my friends and family, and he was home doing what he called "babysitting" his own baby. I now understand how and why abusers attempt to isolate their victims from their support (recall I had a supporting family). So, by this time, I was starting to feel weary, tired of the fighting, and confused because my heart was still attached to him. However, something deep within me was telling me, "You have got to get yourself and your children out of this situation." I used to just sit and cry; the once bubbly girl had become this quiet and shy, young woman who was afraid of her surroundings.

Let me tell you: No matter how many friends you are talking to and the advice they give, the best person you can go to is God! He will hear your cries and pleads, and God says, "Come unto me, I will give you rest."

I had to leave my apartment, so I went to my aunt's house since Baby Daddy had some type of access to my place. We also had a daughter together who he'd come pick up, but I made some changes so I was never alone with him again. You see, he grew up with my four cousins; therefore, he knew how they all would fight to protect their own, so trust and do believe when you ask God to guide you, He will do just that, if you harken unto His Word.

After some time, he was no longer acting crazy and things were going really well. I had been out of high school for two years, and I decided I was ready to go to college. I started taking a few night classes at a business school, and during this time, my grandfather fell very ill. When the day came that I learned my grandfather was never going home again, that I was never going to hold his hand or hear his deep voice call my name again, I was heartbroken. My world was messed up enough, so I did not know how I was going to make it without the strength of my grandfather, but I kept remembering those words, "But this too shall pass." Even though I was going through so much turmoil, God had placed a set up for me.

I found my passion and gift of nursing during one of my roughest times. The last conversation I had with my grandfather consisted of him asking me, "What are you going to do with your life? Why are you still with that boy?" He just wanted so much for me, and I was at a point in my life that I was searching for something. I wanted to be loved, and I was bursting with so much love to give. That's when I gave my life to Christ. I was tired of running, and I also decided to go to nursing school at WSSU. Well, Baby Daddy was not having that! I could go to any school but WSSU. Because of the chance of me being around young, strong and confident black men, he had actually forbidden me to go there. However, he was not paying for me to go to school; I had assistance from the state that paid full tuition for me to attend college, and I was definitely taking the opportunity to change me and my children's lives. Since he had returned to his old ways (though they truly never left), I decided to stick to a routine once school started. I was no longer working, so I would stay at my aunt's house mostly during the week and go to my place on weekends when school was out.

One Saturday night, I was out and did not feel like driving back across town, so I headed home for a few hours of sleep before church. I was by myself, and since he and I were no longer talking on a regular basis, I was not expecting any issues. Well, to my surprise, I was awakened after about an hour of sleep with him standing over me with this creepy, devilish grin. I was his, and he was not letting me go. I remember asking him how he got in and how he even knew I was there. I later found out that he was doing drive-bys at my house and my aunt's house...*tick, tick*...clocking me.

Next thing I knew, it was on like a pot of neck bones. I was in the battle for my life, but he was laughing like The Joker. He jumped on me and began trying to pull my clothes off. The more I said no, the more he laughed and kept trying. I somehow got out from under him and the fight intensified. The more I hit and threw objects at him, he just kept laughing and saying things like I was his, I wasn't going anywhere, and he could do whatever he wanted to me because I belonged to him.

To this day, I do not understand his behavior. Why torture a person all night with fighting, breaking up furniture, etc.? He enjoyed that control. I finally was able to get into my daughter's room and lock the door, and I prayed. I had no phone, no access to get out, and he told me, "You got to come pass me to get out." What was I to do, but call on the name of the Lord? I sat in a corner on my daughter's bed too afraid to close my eyes, and I prayed for God to help me.

Come sun up, my prayers were answered because when my aunt did not see me at her house for church on Sunday morning, her spirit told her something was just not right. She came looking for me, and she came with her sons as backup. When they got there, I could not even let them in because I was that afraid he would grab me if I opened that bedroom door. My cousin came in through the same window that I guess Baby Daddy came in because once I heard my family's voices, I opened the bedroom door. He walked right out the house like nothing happened, and there I was left there distraught from the entire incident—black and bruised, hurt and scared. I reported the incident. However, I dropped it later on for my daughter's sake. But I knew from that moment on, there was no more attachment to Baby Daddy; he was just that...my "baby daddy," and that too did pass.

All those signs I chose not to see earlier in the relationship were leading up to that last rumble. I had reached that point that enough was enough. Thank God I made it out alive. Each situation we choose to brush off as just being light and make excuses for, we are just enabling them and placing ourselves and loved ones at risk for harm.

If you recognize any of the signs I mentioned or are otherwise afraid of your significant other, please seek out help. If you do not have family support, there are local agencies and self-help groups that will assist victims in recognizing signs, get support, and plan for their safety. I recommend starting with the National Resource Center on Domestic Violence's website http://nrcdv.org, or call the National Domestic Violence Hotline at 1-800-787-3224. If in *immediate* need, call 911. The life that you save may be yours!

Marice

4

I Am Beautiful

TAMICA JONES

I was 31 years old, transitioning out of the Army after serving eight years. I took a governmental service job, which is where I met him. He worked on post at Ft. Meade as the security guard where I worked. We would always start the work day with a "hello" and a smile before clocking in. He was always so polite, charming and very quiet unless spoken to. It was nice when I would see him at work. Then we began bumping into each other outside of work, like at the mall and different restaurants. You would think we were planning it or something, but we really never discussed our after work activities. I thought maybe we just lived close to each other. One day, in the break room, I remember walking in as he was watching Sports Center, as he always did. He looked at me, smiled and looked back at the TV. As I was getting ready to walk out with my lunch, he asked me if I would go out on a date with him. Without a pause, I said yes.

After that first date, we became very close—always together or on the phone. He was so sweet: flowers, candy and cards, just because. We would go out dancing, to dinner, and play video games. When I moved into my new apartment, he helped me put things together and fixed things that would break. He would wash my car, go get things I needed without complaint; he was almost too good to be true. We would plan bump-in dates so the kids could meet each other and we could do things as a family. I felt like everything was happening so fast, but it felt wonderful, and I was happy. After six months of dating, he asked me to marry him on Valentine's Day, and I said yes.

Thank God that never happened. I began seeing signs in his statements and actions, but something in me just needed and wanted to believe this relationship could work so badly that I ignored the signs. God was trying to tell me something, but I just didn't listen. He would say he didn't like that my job as a social worker had so many late hours, or that I had to work on the weekends. Baltimore was dangerous; he said he just wanted me to be safe. I thought that was cute until he started calling wanting to know where I was, when I would be getting home, and to call him when I got there. He would complain about my clothes, making comments like, "You should dress more like a mother." Then he started buying my clothes. He would lean over or act like he was hugging me from behind just to see my phone and would complain about me going on trips or outings with my girlfriends. After we moved in together, he would check my phone while I was in the shower and ask me who I was talking to while I was on the phone. He also told me I needed to get a job that allowed me to have the weekends off so we could spend them together. I then saw that things were getting worse. At first, I blamed his changes on life events and lack of money. Sometimes, I would even blame myself for him getting so angry. I thought if I did more, it would take the pressure off and he would be nicer, but that was just an excuse I was making for his behavior.

The beginning of the end started when I took on a second job. We needed the money because it wasn't coming in like it used to. His ex-wife was getting child support in the amount of $1,054 for one child. He had just gotten laid off, and he took a job making half of what he used to make. Our rent was $1,500 and the list of bills went on and on. One day, I arrived home five minutes late from what he called my allotted time to get home. This was the first incident of physical abuse. He fractured my leg. After the first incident, I thought, "This is not him. He didn't mean to. I'll be on time and do what he asks since he's not asking for much. If I do what he is asking, this will not happen again." *How wrong I was.* There were more incidents to follow: black eyes because I was looking at someone too long, slaps and grabbing the wheel while I was driving on the expressway with our infant in the backseat. He'd do those things because I'd pick up my cell phone while he was yelling. By the way, what I call "yelling," he called talking.

The physical abuse soon began with my kids during the times when I wasn't home. He once hit my five-year-old son in the head with a pair of football cleats because he forgot to take them to practice. My oldest would jump up in the middle of the night to help me fight him off of me because he was just in the mood to fight. I began to live with many fears, walking on eggshells so that I would not upset him. I feared the physical harm and injuries, and I also feared that I had caused all of the problems. When I would think I was ready to leave the abusive situation, my fears would only increase: thoughts of starting all over again with my children, telling people that knew me I had failed again, and thinking maybe he would one day treat someone like I deserved to be treated. I felt like it was my duty to stay and that if I loved him enough, he would stop. So I stayed, thinking things would get better, but they didn't.

Then came that Sunday morning that was unlike any other morning. It was a fight just to get to church. It started in the house with him talking about how I had to be sleeping with someone in the church because I was there every Tuesday night and Sunday morning. He didn't know church was my place of peace. The yelling started downstairs as I was looking for the baby's bag. He got up in my face and pushed me, then followed it with a slap. To stop it from getting worse, I ran into one of the three rooms we had in our basement. *What in the world have I gotten myself into? Why am I putting up with this crazy stuff? I'm too old for this! This is not how I wanted my kids to grow up. Is this really what God has for me?* Those were the questions going through my head as I used my body to barricade the door. He was trying to come through as he shouted the same profanities that he had repeated so many times before. I could repeat them by heart and in my sleep. In that moment, my mind started doing a review as the tears ran down my face. I knew, in that moment, something had to change. I had to find a way to break my silence, let go of my shame, let go of my pride, and encourage myself so that I could live and not die. I had to get out of that relationship. It wasn't healthy for me or my children, so I knew I had to come up with a plan.

I felt like I could get that plan if I could get to church because my blessings were at church waiting on me—not the building, but the church on the inside of me, where I needed God to be. I knew God was the key to unlock the plan that He had placed inside of me because He didn't build me for that. I needed the encouragement that only comes from the word of God; I needed life. I couldn't call friends and family. All I had was God, so I began speaking to myself. I told myself enough is enough. I began to say, "This is not my fault," even though I didn't understand why it was happening to me. Proverbs 3:5 states, "Trust in the LORD with all your heart and do not lean on your own understanding." I said to myself, God made me the head and not the tail. Deuteronomy 28:13 says, "The LORD will make you the head, not the tail. If you pay attention to the commands of the LORD your God that I give you this day and carefully follow them, you will always be at the top, never at the bottom."

I told myself that God was hearing my cries and that He didn't leave me, I left Him. All I had to do was repent and get it right with God. When I started speaking those words to myself, I noticed that he must have gotten tired of kicking and yelling at the door. I heard the door close and his truck start up outside. I grabbed my stuff and my two youngest, and ran to get in my van. I thought I was in the clear.

After I closed my van door and put on my seatbelt, as I was talking on the phone with my girlfriend, I started yelling. In a blink of an eye, I saw him getting ready to ram his truck head on into my van, and that is exactly what he did. Then he got out of his truck and came towards my van. I told him that I had called the police and that they were on their way. When he heard me say that, he got into his truck and drove away. I knew that was my chance to get to church. I had a heavy heart at that moment, but I knew everything was going to be okay. I knew God had not forgotten me because He had a plan for me, and this was not it. With my bumper hanging off my van, I made it to church. I walked into church with my two youngest children and ate the word up that morning as if it was just for me. I now had a plan, and it was coming straight from the Lord.

Now when you get a plan from the Lord, there is no way you can fail as long as you allow God to order your steps. When you get to the *enough is enough* place, grab a piece of paper and start writing down what God is saying to you word-for-word. Write down what your self-worth and joy looks like to you. In order for this plan to work, you have to first forgive yourself and understand that this is not your fault. There was nothing you could have done to save or control another person. You have to understand that hurt people hurt other people, and the only person you can change is yourself. Another thing you need to do is find out what your legal rights are. You may have to get a protection order that will allow your abuser to still see his child(ren), if you have kids together, but stay away from you. You need to seek counseling for yourself and the kids, if you have children. If you cannot afford counseling, there is free counseling at your local DSS office or local battered women's program. They will keep you safe from your abuser and help you start looking for another place to stay if you need it.

At the time of abuse, as it is happening, you feel lost and as if there is no end in sight. Take it one day at a time and slowly, but surely, with God's help, you will begin to put the pieces of your life back together. It requires you to speak life to yourself every day, even on the days that you don't feel like getting up or when you don't feel worthy to get up. Repeat Roman 8:37, "No, despite all these things, overwhelming victory is ours through Christ, who loved us." Also quote Deuteronomy 31:6, which says, "Be strong and courageous. Do not be afraid or terrified because of them, for the LORD your God goes with you; he will never leave you nor forsake you."

You have to believe you are worth the price that Jesus paid on the cross for you. There is a purpose in your pain. I know it's hard when you are in your storm, but you can do it. You're not dead, and what doesn't kill you makes you stronger.

Tamica

Broken Barriers

Focus towards heart's melody consumed in me,

Transparent message held eyes captive to clearly see,

Hardness of walls formed a dark lonely hiding place,

Woman altered from child dressed in handcrafted lace,

Understand my strength's existence that visually abides inches deep;

Sweet low song of scars yield painful souls to passionately weep,

Declaring termination of generational female revile,

Sing the sonata from within love extended in denial,

Breaking all barriers acknowledging my honest worth's merit,

Awaiting her desiring acceptance of devotional diamond's carat.

- Spicee Gray

5

I Am Healed

TRINITA WILLIAMS

As a kid, I always dreamed of the perfect wedding. I wanted a big wedding and a happily ever after. I wanted forever. Then reality kicked in, life took over, and I forgot all about that childhood dream. Life taught me that just because you think you know a person does not mean that you really do. My ex-husband and I knew each other since we were kids. In our late teenage years, we became the best of friends. A couple of years after graduating from high school, we started dating. We were that couple everyone loved. As we started spending more time together, our relationship grew stronger, and we decided to get an apartment together. Life was great; I was moving in to my first apartment with my two best friends at the time.

In all relationships, couples argue and stop speaking, so I wasn't worried when we started arguing. We never stayed upset and the arguments weren't serious. We started talking about marriage and, a few months later, we found out that I was pregnant with our first child. We were both excited and decided to hold off on the wedding plans since I was sick all of the time and couldn't keep anything down. Things started to change between my best friend and I, so my ex-husband and I decided that it would be best if we moved out. My mom wanted me to come back home, since I was always sick. *Man, I don't know what I would do without my family.*

My ex-husband worked at the Base Exchange with my mother, and he was also a DJ at the base club, so he was always out. I didn't think anything was wrong with that. I was focusing on work and planning for our first child. I really think that I was so happy to be home with my family that nothing else really mattered.

In August of '93, our friends and family had a baby shower for us. My ex-husband's mom and sister came to celebrate with us. We were having so much fun, and it was so nice to have my family and friends laughing and talking to his mom and sister. I remember standing next to my dad while he was talking to them. My ex-husband came over, and his mother called his name so that she could talk to him. All I remember is him yelling at her in front of me, my dad and everyone at the shower. My mouth dropped because I had never heard him talk to his mom like that. I will never forget the look on her face. She just looked at me and gave me a hug and told me and my dad that she was leaving. As I watched his mom and sister walk away, I was trying to register what just happened. I could see how disappointed and upset my dad was. My ex-husband walked over to my dad and started talking like nothing happened. I remember my dad telling him that he was wrong and that family is very important to him, and that he better make sure that he apologizes to his mother. I don't know if he ever did because it never came up again.

After that, I noticed little things, and we started arguing a little more than usual. In September of '93, we welcomed our daughter into the world. I remember him holding our daughter for the first time. He was smiling and singing to her, then his pager went off. The next thing we knew, he was forcing the baby in his sister's arm, knowing that she was scared to hold her. When he walked out of the room, his sister and I just looked at each other wondering what was going on. He returned to the room saying that the club was calling to see if he could help the DJ turn on the equipment.

I stayed with my parents for a few months after having my daughter. My sister and brother were such a big help. Then, in January '94, we went to city hall and got married. I was the one that wanted to go to city hall. Yes, I had always dreamed of my wedding day, and, no, it wasn't at city hall. We had so much going on, trying to move into our new apartment. Plus, I was back at work and just wasn't in the mood to plan a wedding. I was also pregnant with our second child and feeling really sick. Things had been going well for a while, or at least I thought so. Our daughter was keeping us really busy, and she was such a daddy's girl. He started working more and doing private parties. I wasn't driving yet, but I used my tax returns to purchase a car so we would be able to get back and forth.

The arguing started up again, and then the late nights started. He would say that he had a party to DJ and that it ended late. Then he started hanging out all night and not coming home. When I would ask him where he was, he would start yelling and name-calling. Now I knew something was wrong. I was wondering if he'd lost his damn mind because we never talked to each other like that. I started hearing from friends of ours that he was on the base hanging out with some military chick and her friend. At this point, I was very pregnant and trying my best to keep it together. We were at Burger King on the base when the young lady walked in with her son. The look on both of their faces was how I knew that she was the one that people were talking about. He tried to act like nothing was going on. Even though I had no proof, I knew something was up when he mentioned that he liked her tattoo. I remembered when my sister and I went to get matching tattoos, and he said how he hated women with tattoos and kept putting me down for it. He was still making rude comments about mine and now he had the nerve to sit in my face talking about how nice this girl's tattoo was.

A week or so later, he ended up staying out all night again. I heard that he spent the night at the military chick's house, and that the friend was there too. I was so upset, and I was trying so hard to keep it together. I didn't understand how everything had fallen apart. The day that I went into labor with our second child, we had gotten into a big argument. I was at work when he called me, but I can't remember what we were arguing over; I just knew that I was really upset. I was sitting at my desk when I felt this unbelievable pain. The pain kept getting stronger, and I was in the office alone with a high school intern. I remember saying, "God please don't let me go into labor in this office right now. I can't leave the intern here by herself."

Then my Chief walked in, and I jumped up and said, "Chief, I have to go." Before he could say anything, I was out the door. I tried to call my ex-husband, but he wasn't at work, and he wasn't answering his phone. I went to the base, and he was getting ready to get on the ferry. We ended up going to the hospital, and our second daughter was born that night. My parents weren't there with me this time, but my sister and my aunt were there. I was so happy to have my family with me because they always make things so much better. The hospital discharged me the next day, but I had to promise to come back the following day so the baby could get blood work done.

Things were getting so crazy now. This man that was once my best friend was turning into a complete stranger. What was I going to do? I couldn't leave because I had two kids, and I was not going to be able to take care of them on my own. I knew my family and friends would support me in whatever I decided to do, but I didn't want my friends and family to know how miserable I was. So I walked around with my fake smile, staying in routine and feeling myself slipping away.

When my parents and brother moved to Seattle, I felt very sad. My sister joined the military and was stationed in Connecticut. Thank God I still had my aunt and cousins close by. I tried to work on my marriage, but it takes two to make it work. My ex-husband was more concerned with impressing all these teenage kids and pretending that he was some big shot with all these cars. He started running up credit card bills, renting cars so that everyone would think that he had multiple cars. Then he was hanging out all night with his single friends, pretending like his wife and kids weren't at home. I felt like I was dealing with a little kid. My mom sent for my daughters for a few months. My parents had missed the girls so much, and my mom wanted to give us a chance to work on our marriage.

Instead of working on our marriage, he took this as a way to hang out more. We began to live separate lives. Thanksgiving came, and we were supposed to go to my aunt's house for dinner, but he decided to take the car and go out to dinner with his friends. I was left home by myself and had to call my aunt and tell her that I wasn't feeling well. I don't think she believed me, but she never questioned it. While my daughters were in Seattle, my brother got real sick and the doctors didn't think he was going to make it. I ended up flying out, not knowing what was going to happen. Initially, I was hurt by him not wanting to come with me, but he didn't even call to see how his daughters were doing since they were there, so why would he go with me to see about my brother? He was busy hanging out with his friends and trying to tear me down. When I returned home from Seattle, I went straight to work from the airport. I was so tired, but I didn't want to go home. I didn't even tell him when my flight was coming in; I just asked one of my co-workers to pick me up from the airport.

That Christmas, my mother came to visit and to bring my daughters home. I was so happy my sister came, and one of our childhood friends came with her husband and daughter. All of the women had colds, but we still had fun. We started feeling better, but my mom couldn't shake her cold. When she returned to Seattle, my dad took her to the doctor where we found out that she had cancer. I didn't know how to handle that news, and I had absolutely no support at home. I turned to my friends and family who helped me keep it together. May of '99, I went to visit my mother for the last time. I remember calling home trying to find out where my girls were and learning that he had them staying at all of these people's houses while he hung out all night. I couldn't enjoy my visit with my mother because I didn't know where my girls were.

When I returned home from Seattle, I was so happy to see my daughters and knew it was time for me to get out of this marriage. In June of '99, my dad called me at 5:26 a.m. to tell me that my mother had passed. I couldn't believe it; I had just called the hospital Friday night, and my dad had said that she was resting. I just dropped the phone and started packing my suitcase. I was going to get my mother because she couldn't be gone. This couldn't be happening. I needed her, she was my rock. I remember him grabbing the phone and talking to my dad. When he hung up, he looked at me and said, "What are you doing? You look stupid, Tre.'" I called my aunt and just broke down. That day, I couldn't get out of the bed, and he left me home alone with the kids because "he had a party to DJ." Thank God for family. My aunt and cousins came over and helped with the girls because I was no good to anyone. They ended up staying the night, and the next morning when my ex-husband came home, my aunt took the girls home with her. It took me a while, but I finally got myself together to make it to Seattle for my mom's funeral. He came, but only because I reminded him that my mother was always good to him, even though he was an ass.

1999 was a bad year for me. So much happened, but that's another story. Needless to say we finally got divorced, and he remarried the trick that he was fooling around with when I was visiting my mother. I found out about that after they were married. He never tried to see his children and has refused to pay child support and is currently in arrears over $15,000.00.

I think that the first sign was my baby shower when he cursed out his mother. You know what they say, "If a man doesn't respect his mother, he won't respect his wife." Then there was the constant disrespect. I have to say that if it wasn't for my family and friends, I wouldn't be who I am today, and my girls wouldn't be who they are today. My family taught me to be a strong, independent woman, and because of that, I was able to raise my girls to be strong, independent women.

I did remarry and have that wedding I always wanted. He was great and he loved my girls like they were his own. I thought it would last forever, but it didn't work out that way. In this marriage, I suffered the worst verbal and emotional abuse. If I had been a weaker woman, I would've committed suicide. Yes, it was that bad. Words hurt, but I'll save that story for another day. What I learned in this marriage is that broken people will rip you apart so that they can feel better about themselves. Although he wasn't a good husband, he is a good father to our two kids and my/our two daughters.

Trinita

6 I Am a Conqueror

KRISTIN MANGUM

I am thankful and blessed to know what the true meaning of love is. I was born in the early '80s into a family of young parents who didn't want the responsibility of a child. In the same breath, I love the family who adopted me and gave me unconditional love. Thus, I've developed a different outlook on life. While growing up, my family used to tell me "I'm selling myself." I was involved in many activities such as church, a dance team, etc. My only accomplishment was fitting in with my peers. I was the oldest amongst my friends, and I was the only virgin as well. Truth be told, I was still a virgin because I was scared to have sex. Therefore, I had a few boyfriends. I let everyone believe I lost my virginity at twelve, although I really lost it at sixteen, because I didn't want to be seen as a nerd. Losing my virginity shined light on the fact that sometimes I had no clue on what I was doing in my life.

After the first taste from my sexual experience, I was intrigued. My urge to have sex deepened so much that I would skip school, even church, to have sex. I would do anything I could do to find a companion for the moment.

The results of my sexual activities reflected on my popularity. I was known as the girl that had it going on for herself. This was until I met a guy I knew I was going to marry, and that made me change for the better. I began to lose myself in a man, who later became the father of my oldest daughter. It took a year of being with this man for me to conceive my daughter. When we were involved, there was no more school for me. In fact, I was staying out all night with him, and in the midst of everything, I forgot what was going on in my family.

One afternoon while my father was helping my uncle fix his tractor, something went wrong. To this day, we do not know how a spark ignited, and my father was caught on fire from head to toe. He was in the hospital's burn unit for weeks with second- and third-degree burns. I didn't even go to the hospital to see him. When he came home, I did not help him nor my mother, and I was not even there for my little sister. I was still following this man. It had gotten so bad, I would let him in my room through the window. He often hid under my bed during the day and on the bed at night. I thought my parents did not know until one day the sheriff pulled up and served him with second-degree trespassing papers. At that time, I couldn't believe my parents would do such a thing. I was so mad at them that I did not even sit in the trial. I did, however, testify against my family.

I ended up breaking a grown man's heart by keeping my pregnancy a secret. In the first couple months of my pregnancy, I did not gain a lot of weight. It wasn't until my ultrasound appointment came in the mail that my secret came out. I could not even look my father in the eye. I just said, "Sir, I am." My father still did not give up on his little girl though. He took me to my high school and asked what I could do in order to graduate. My principal gave me a great offer to come back one semester to finish school. I was in the twelfth grade then, and I told my principle no thank you to his offer. I dropped out of school in April, which was the last year of high school. I still chose my man over everything.

As time went by, I got bigger and bigger during my pregnancy. I gained one hundred pounds. I couldn't even sleep in a bed or go see my boyfriend. He couldn't even come see me like I wanted him to. While at home alone, I tried to get back in church and became very close to the Serenity Prayer. I did not understand my life or choices I had made, but I was influenced to name my little girl Serenity. The birth of my baby girl was the beginning of a new experience. Flashing back to it, my daughter's heart rate could not take my contractions. I was in labor for fourteen hours and ended up having a C-section. I remember her being so beautiful and perfect. I just knew my life was complete. This was not the case, however, because I was still dealing with her father. I stayed at home with my little one for six weeks, while her father was gone by eight o'clock each night. I did not want my daughter spending the night with her father alone.

After my child was born, it was time for me to move out and get a job. I had an education, but no high school diploma. Plus, I did not have any work experience, but I was lucky enough to get hired at the Kirby Vacuum service company.

My job entailed me going door to door selling a huge vacuum. I never made any money, and what made matters worse was that I was the only girl on the team. Thus, I referred my child's father to my job, and he became an employee. I thought he could help us receive a good source of income. Unfortunately, all he did was flirt with the ladies whose house we went in to sell vacuums. From this point on, I decided to not get played for a fool anymore and move on.

My child's grandmother convinced me that I was young and had my whole life ahead of me. I believed her, and I let my baby live with my family. I ended up moving in with one of the guys I worked with. He was cute, no kids, and was a top seller. I just knew he was going to take care of me. At this time, it was just all about me. I saw my daughter once a month or when I went home to see my parents, acting like everything was okay. Meanwhile, I was home smoking and drinking with a great sex life. My new boo did things like furnish my whole apartment to take care of me. We had so much fun together, and his family was so nice. Everyone kept saying, "You better do well by her," and I did not know what they meant by that until one night my friend came over. We started smoking and drinking when a guy came to the door, and there he was, the cute weed man. He asked my friend, "What's up with your friend," referring to me, and as he said that, my man walked in the door. I did not think anything about that confrontation until that night. My boo was in the bathroom, I lying across my bed, and he asked me, "So you sleeping with that nigga?" Without a second to speak, he was on top of me punching me in my face, saying,

"I will kill you if you ever try to play me." Feeling helpless, I just rolled over and cried. At that moment, I told myself that he did not mean it.

The next morning, I woke up to flowers and breakfast. I was thankful that he was okay, but scared all at the same time. I could not let him see how scared I was though. I knew I would not do anything else to piss him off, or at least I thought. The physical abuse became more frequent over time. All he needed was some Paul Mason to give him some liquid courage. Every morning, it was, "I'm sorry. It's my fault," and after a while, I would believe it. I would not even let my girlfriend come over anymore. I would go over there and make sure I was home at least an hour before he got home. The house was cleaned, dinner was cooked, and I did everything in my power to keep his hands off me. Fortunately, he calmed down from the physical abuse, and I put my guards down. Maybe that is what he wanted—for me to trust him again. It could be the fact that he did not want me to tell his family or ask questions about that comment they made to him when we first met. I forgave him, but, in the back of my mind, I knew he was not all the way there in the head and that what he was doing was not right at all.

My friends, feeling left out, came by one day asking a lot of questions. That made me nervous for a couple of reasons: What if he came home early? What do they know? I told them I was fine and did not need them all up in my business. One girl asked, "He's hitting you, isn't he?"

I replied, "Girl, no, I don't know what you're talking about. My boo loves me, and he'll never hit me." I disregarded my friends, "Don't you get me mixed up in your lives! Now get out my house!"

After that conversation I just sat in my living room crying in silence. Saying the only prayer I knew, well the only one that made a difference in my life, the Serenity Prayer: "God grant me the serenity to accept the things I cannot change; courage to change the things I can; and wisdom to know the difference. Amen."

I got off my couch, put on my clothes, and called for my little girl. A lot of time had passed. In fact, she was almost one, potty trained, walking and talking. I had seen her a couple times during these crazy years of my life, but today I needed my baby girl. I left a note for my boyfriend that I was going to get my little girl for the weekend, and I would talk to him later. In the midst of this, he had made plans of his own. He invited one of my close friends over and one of his homeboys. It is not a party without liquor. Therefore, Mr. Paul Mason was present. When I arrived home, my living room was smoked out with ashes on the floor and bottles of beer everywhere. I just took my baby, ran upstairs, and closed the door. She was so happy to see me, and I was to see her, but I was scared as hell and ready to go. I heard footsteps coming upstairs and started panicking. I started putting her stuff in the closet. The door opened, and I held my little girl so tight, she started crying. He opened the door and reached for her. I did not want to let my baby go, but I knew it could only be worse if I didn't. Thank God he calmed down. He began playing with her, but then he took her down the hall to her room and sat her on the bed, telling me to not be rude because we have guests. I inhaled deeply and dropped my head and went downstairs, but not without saying, "I'm not going to stay long. Serenity needs me!" He gave me a look that almost made me fall down the steps. I greeted everyone and took a shot. I had about ten minutes of small talk, and Serenity started crying. I jumped to get my baby, but "my boo" insisted on having her. He fixed her bottle and went upstairs. He said, "Keep drinking with your friends." I said to myself, "Okay, why not? He's being very nice." *The feeling of enjoying myself, I could get used to this.* The liquor bottle was empty, and my friend and I were drunk, so I let everyone spend the night. Not thinking tonight would be the night to remember.

I took a shower before getting into our bed where Serenity was lying so peacefully. I could not wait to lie there beside her and smell her baby breath. I love that smell. My boo crawled into bed hours later and tried to have sex with me while my baby girl was lying next to me. I refused and told him to stop playing with me while the baby was in the bed. He got mad and woke her up. At this point, I was pissed, so I took her in the other room and got in the bed. He gave me enough time to put her to sleep and fall asleep myself. Suddenly, all hell broke loose as he started choking me. I woke up in defense. There was a punch to the face, which made me black out for a second. I kept hearing Serenity crying and him calling me everything but the child of God. As he pulled my pants off in front of my little girl, I tried my best to get away from him. I told myself to calm down, and I performed oral sex. As soon as he put his penis in my mouth, I bit it. He fell to his knee. I grabbed my baby and took off running to the bathroom. He recovered and started beating down the door. I saw it was coming off the hinges, so I looked under the bathroom sink. There I saw a bottle of Windex, and I opened the door to spray the cleaner in his face and started running down stairs. I looked to my left and saw my friend and his friend having sex on the couch. They didn't even stop, much less look my way. I did not care; all I heard were footsteps coming downstairs. I made it out the back door, and I saw that, across the street, my neighbor's bedroom light was on. I screamed, "Help! Please someone help me!" My neighbor turned off the light and closed their window. My baby girl and I were laying on the wet grass. With a size ten and a half Timberland boot on my back, he pissed on me and my baby. I tried so hard to keep her covered, but when I moved, he pressed harder in my back. I just laid there in my tears and his urine. He just left us there, and I think we laid there all night until the sun came up. I didn't want to go in; I just wanted this moment to stop. I do not remember how or what really happened next because I was in and out of consciousness.

Someone got in contact with the office and got in touch with my emergency contact which was my little sister, and she arrived with the Roxboro police. The rookie cop came and said that there was no sign of abuse and left. My sister could not believe this and asked for his superior. Mr. Whitfield became my hero when he came and took him away. I was relieved my sister looked at me and said, "Why Krissy!? Why Krissy!? You don't deserve this. Serenity doesn't, either." I dropped my head and went into my house. My company was still sitting in my living room like nothing even happened. I looked at them and asked why they did not help me. His friend replied that it was none of his business. To that, I reacted by telling him to get out of my business, which was my house.

My child's father was only in jail for 72 hours, and I did not have a ride to court to testify, so they let him free. I told him and his family that they were not allowed in my home. That same dumb friend came by to get his clothes. I felt relieved and alive again, without the thought of him returning home, which was foolish of me. I was hanging out talking to my friend about that guy who came to my house months ago to serve her. I heard a knock at the door and without recognizing the person, I invited them in. It was him with a knife in his hand to kill me where I stood. All I could hear was my friend asking, "Who is this guy?" Not responding, she knew to call someone, hopefully the police. Instead, she called that boy who showed up with a gang of guys and guns. This made that grown man run up out of the hood. He has not been back.

I don't believe I saw any sign to know what was coming. There was no mental abuse or name calling. He didn't even have a temper; he was a nice guy. His upper was brown liquor. It gave him ego like never before and made him mean, evil, and incoherent to what was going on. After our last fight, with my little girl in my arms, I would say enough was enough, but that isn't really true. Almost twelve years has passed, and I still deal with emotional abuse. I have been looking for love in all the wrong places. I fell in with a girl who I knew would love me forever, but, because I was a tenant and just wanted someone to love me, I missed all of her signs, too.

The best thing was finding God. My cosmetology teacher was a pastor and could read me like a book, so besides teaching me how to rope, she taught me how and why to fast. My first one was seven days and the next one was 30 days. I joined La'Ticia's #SpeakLife Challenge, and it was a true eye opener. I met some wonderful people and learned that I wasn't the only one dealing with all these issues. I also fell in love with a quote and think that showed how I was feeling. I posted it as a screenshot and put it on a sticky note.

I can't tell you when enough is enough or how to get out, but I can tell you that God is an amazing man who will never leave nor forsake you. He heals all wounds and doesn't judge. He is the best person to talk and cry to, and He welcomes you with open arms. Counseling helps and domestic violence shelters help, but without God, those things and places don't mean anything.

Kristin

Fist Full of Tears

The mind is racing compacted with trials of life,

Heartaches sending blows pulsating levels
from one's strife,

Her soul is darkened from shadows lurking all round,

Lips frozen stiff, restricting developmental form of sound,

Questioning paths bad seed from whence one sow,

Wounds and scars which is of deserving,
she just don't know,

Exhausted: body falls numb on blanketed sand,

Focusing towards dancing ocean waves as an orchestrated
band,

Winds softly massaging her face while it flows swiftly by,

Temporarily comforting her inward spirits as briskly time fly,

Remembering shared time together and joy he bought to
her heart,

Misconception of her words resulted in tearing them apart,

Emptiness fills her life at the silence of his voice,

Being treated as an auctioned valued item withheld from
her choice,

Yearning for his love he kept her placement confused,

Past image of offerings is what drawled her completely amused,

His hand slowly faded as towards love grew even stronger,

The man who hungered her in desire existed no longer,

Spaded cards flipped as the guarded gate opened wide,

Assuming through everything he would remain by one side,

All appears a nightmare for he always imprinted her smile,

In need of his embrace from misconception in distancing mile,

Gradually she gently opens the eyes as inward beginning fears,

Looking down in her hands embraced was a fist full of tears.

- *Spicee Gray*

7

I Am Loved

CHANDRA SOUTHERN

In my family, the women are headstrong and not easily intimidated. If there was ever a fight, you better believe that they never let anyone get the best of them. I adopted that same mentality. I would never start a fight, but you better believe that I didn't back down from one either. I had a tough girl mentality, a huge chip on my shoulder, and if you said one thing to me that I didn't like, I was a firecracker ready to be lit.

I had learned to carry a secret really well. One would never know that I spent most of my preteen and teenage years being sexually abused by an adult family member. He was so loving and charming to others and had open access to me anytime he wanted. His threats to kill me and my family made me suffer from migraines.

I lived in fear of him and what he would do to me if I told. I remember sitting outside at the pool one day talking to a friend that was a boy on the phone, and my mother called and told me to cut up a chicken for dinner before she got home. He sat at the kitchen table watching me as I was struggling to cut up the chicken, which I'd never done before. He got so angry and called me stupid for not knowing how to use the knife properly, but he was really mad about the conversation with the boy. He jumped up, and I thought he was coming for the knife, but instead he took his belt off and hit me with the buckle several times. It hurt so bad I ran to my room and locked myself in until my mom came home. I had this huge bruise that was swollen black and blue on my thigh, and I was limping from the pain. He was gone by the time she came home, but when she asked why I was walking like that, I told her I hurt it at track practice. I still have the faint scar on my thigh today.

It was the spring of 1984; I was still considered the new kid on the block, only having moved there a few months prior. Most of them knew me as the kid with the pool in the backyard. This particular day, as I got off the school bus, one of my neighbors told me he locked his keys in the house. I considered him to be a really cool person and friend. Since I was so skinny, he thought I could probably fit through the window and unlock the door for him. I said, "Sure, why not," and climbed in and opened the door. *Piece of cake.* When he came in, he asked me to stay, and I told him I could not I had to go home and do my homework.

He proceeded to walk toward me and locked the door. That door had multiple locks on it. I asked him what he was doing, and he grabbed my arm and squeezed it, asking for a kiss. I told him, "No, move!" He grabbed me by my neck and pulled me close to him and tried to kiss me again. I tried to fight him off by kicking, biting, scratching, punching, but of course, he was much stronger than me. He picked me up, pinned me to the floor, pulled my pants off, and as I screamed for help, I lost that fight. Back in the day, most of us were latch key kids—no parents at home until after 6:30 p.m. most days. We got out of school at 2:15 p.m., so there was plenty of time for things to happen. I was so exhausted, but as soon as I could, I grabbed my things and ran as fast as I could home. Who could I tell? I couldn't stop shaking like a leaf. I jumped in the shower, cleaned off, looked in the mirror, and said to myself, "This is just something else you have to deal with. Stop crying like a baby and suck it up."

I woke up the next morning, feeling like I had been in a car accident. My arm and wrist hurt from being held and squeezed so hard, my knuckles were sore from punching, and my eyes were puffy from crying myself to sleep. I pulled myself together, and as I walked to the bus stop, there he was, laughing and joking with everyone like nothing at all happened. I felt sick and dirty, like everyone was staring at me, and every time the guys laughed, I thought they were laughing at me. I was very quiet the entire day. My friend KK asked what was wrong with me, and I just said, "Nothing, I will be alright."

After school, KK asked me to wait because she wanted to talk to me. My neighbor looked back at me as if to say you better not say anything. KK asked again what was wrong, and I couldn't hold it in, so I told her, "You can't say anything to anyone." The words spilled out so fast, and all I thought was now someone else knows; they can help to protect me. Wishful thinking. Not even 24 hours later, I got on the bus and was being called names from the back of the bus. He even came and sat in front of me on the bus, staring at me, but wouldn't say anything. I was trapped with nowhere to go. His female cousins would threaten me on the bus every day, and I thought to myself, "The only way they are going to leave me alone is if I fight both of them. Win or lose, at least they will know." I was not scared, but before any blows could be thrown, someone's parent came home early and told all of us to go home.

The next five years, I put all of that drama behind me. I actually started talking to him again since I had to see him every single day, whether at school or home. It was my junior year in high school, and I was walking to work because my car was messed up. I got near the big hill, and I saw this car drive by and pull over in front of me. It was him, my neighbor. He jumped out and said, "Come on, girl. I will give you a ride." I hesitated and my stomach felt funny. I even said, "No, that's okay," but I was thinking after all of that stuff years ago, he would not dare try anything again, so against my gut instinct, I got in.

Not even a block down the street, he turned down a dirt road where construction was being done. I immediately started cussing him out, "Where are we going?" He said he had to turn around because he forgot something at the house and had to go all the way back. I said, "I can walk from here, just let me go. I don't want to be late." I began grabbing at the door handle and tried to jump out, but he grabbed my arm and pulled me back in while he was still driving really fast to the dead end. We were way off down this road, away from cars seeing us from the main street. This time I fought a little harder, putting a dent in the dashboard of the car, busting his lip, and scratching up the side of his neck.

Even after all that, I still lost that battle.

I got out and started walking from all the way down the road. He drove beside me and told me to get back in; he would still take me. I cussed at him the entire way as he made fun of me while he sped up and slowed down several times. I picked up a few rocks and threw them at his car. When I finally made it to the top, I just decided to go home and call out of work, but when I got near my home, to my surprise, I saw the car of my adult abuser. I turned around, dirty and all, and walked to the city bus stop and went to work. When I got to work, my co-workers and ex-boyfriend asked me what was wrong with my hair and why my clothes were dirty. I told them I tripped and fell while walking. Lying to cover up for what was happening to me on a daily basis with my adult abuser was pretty easy at that point.

Fast forward five years and he (now an adult) was arrested for raping his girlfriend's little sister. I think he had to serve about 8-10 years. For years, I blamed myself, saying if I had reported him maybe I could have saved that young lady from a lot of pain and sorrow. I eventually spoke up about the other things that happened to me, but no one was ever punished. They only blamed me and called me a liar. I felt so alone, and I attempted to commit suicide when I was fifteen years old. This was the day I learned that God was really real. I heard His voice and felt His touch on my shoulder, saving my life that day. That day changed my focus, and it led people to my life to help me eventually become a better woman, but I still went through a lot of changes before I realized what was really going on. I may have been ready to physically go to blows if you put your hands on me, but what I had not realized was that emotionally, I allowed men to run my life.

I have been in long term relationships, off and on, since middle school. In each one of them, I bent over backwards for them and felt like I was always on an emotional rollercoaster. My self-esteem at one point was so low that I remember one of them asking me would I consider letting his friends gang bang me. Can you imagine the look on my face? I must admit, I thought about it. Just the thought of knowing that I had actually considered it makes me sick to my stomach today. It never happened, but what if? The same boyfriend told me one time when I thought I could be pregnant to blame it on this other guy I had dated in between our break ups. That showed just how much he really wanted to be in my life, huh? I still didn't see it. We argued through the years, but just couldn't stay away from each other. He cheated on all his other girlfriends to be with me. I thought I was special and the reason we couldn't be boyfriend and girlfriend anymore was because we argued too much.

I tried to permanently cut all ties with him, and one day he locked us in his bedroom and told me there was only one way out. He threw me on the bed and began biting me all over my body until he got to my neck. I remember the pain from his teeth digging into my skin, and every time I moved, there was this deep burning sensation going through my body. All I could do was cry. He told me I would always remember him; he wanted to make sure of that. I was scared and didn't know exactly what that meant, so I used all my strength to push him off me, not realizing that he had pulled a plug of skin out of my neck with his teeth. I moved the chair from in front of the door and ran out of the house and down the street with no shoes. I left my bag and all. He stood at the door and teased me with my car keys, telling me I still couldn't go anywhere unless I walked. Eventually, after about 30 minutes, his mom came home and made him give me all my stuff, and I left. Every time I look in the mirror, I can see the scar on my neck.

I remember thinking that I was head over heels for another guy. I did his homework, washed his clothes, and spent money on him. This dude cheated on me so many times I lost count, but I thought I was special because I was the one he called his girlfriend in public. We would break up several times, but we could not stand the thought of seeing the other dating someone else. I even walked up on him sitting in a car with some girl, and he still denied that anything was going on. One day, I went to see him, and since someone else let me in, I caught him on the phone talking to an "old" girlfriend, telling her he loved her. I was crushed! He got mad at me, accusing me of listening in on his conversation and being sneaky by not saying anything. In the heat of the argument, he pushed me as he walked away. I pushed back, and he turned around and slapped me. I faded to black and snapped. He tried to run up some steps, and I was right behind him and yanked him down by his shirt collar and stood over him and told him if he ever in his life put his hands on me, I would kill him. I put a long scar on the back of his neck that's probably still there to this day. We had several pushing and shoving matches after that for years, but he never lifted his hands up to hit me again.

However, I allowed him to continue to mentally manipulate me. I was so stressed by an incident that I considered to be the straw that broke the camel's back, the ultimate betrayal. One day at work, my head was hurting so bad I could barely see, so I left work early. I laid down at about 3 p.m. and woke up to this pain so sharp that it grabbed me in my chest. It felt like someone had reached in and was twisting and stabbing me in my heart all at the same time. I couldn't breathe. I tried to call friends who lived close by, but no one was home. I wouldn't call 911 because I feared that when you got in the back of an ambulance you wouldn't come out alive, so I actually drove myself to the emergency room for chest pains while hyperventilating. I prayed and prayed, "Lord, please guide me to this hospital." It was cold and raining, and I couldn't see that well, but God! They could not say for sure if it was a mild stroke, panic attack, or what. The next few days, I could not go to work because my left side of my arm and face was numb, felt twisted, and I had headaches and blurred vision. I had to ask myself how much more was I going to take and why I continued to live in misery and anger. I had to put an end to all the hurt and pain he had caused me over the years, but, because of my limited sense of self-worth, I continued settling for less, allowing myself to be emotionally shattered and verbally assaulted.

I found myself right back in another dysfunctional relationship. This one would tell me what I should and should not wear by making little comments like, "Why are you wearing that. It doesn't look right," or "Why are you wearing your hair that way?" or "Why don't you wear heels like she has on, that looks nice on her?" I would go and change outfits to something that I didn't really like, but as long as it made him happy, I didn't care. He even went as far as tell me who to be friends with. He would make comments like, "You need to be careful hanging with her, she seems shady" and "You don't know anything about that person."

When I would take on different jobs, there would be comments like, "You are spending too much time at work. When are you going to find time for me?" I would work less to just be with him. I even turned down a great career opportunity because he didn't think it was lady-like to get free training at night since women should not work late at night unless they are in the strip club.

Little by little, I realized I was not living my life for me. I don't like drama, so I became a people pleaser to keep the peace.

One day, I remember getting a phone call telling me that one of my family members had been murdered by her spouse. He had been verbally abusive over the years with idle threats, but this day, he followed through. This was a wakeup call for me. Believe people when they tell you what they are going to do. I thought, "Wow! That could have been me." I was on edge after that with relationships, but somehow I still allowed myself to get caught up with partners who didn't value me because I didn't value me. I felt less than trash. I had been used up and abused. That was the day I decided that no man would ever stress me out so much that I would die for it. One day, I looked in the mirror and said to myself, "Who are you?" I didn't recognize me. I called and asked one of my BFFs what she saw in me. She has always been very honest and blunt, but didn't want to hurt my feelings. She told me she didn't recognize me, I had changed.

We all know that when you are in something, it's hard for you to see it yourself. I had to take my power back and stop allowing men to continue to hurt me. I deserved better. I became a very active volunteer in my community, which developed my foundation for giving back to others, leadership and public speaking. I had an awesome mentor who I can still call today if I need to run some ideas by her. She helped me see the positive side of things that life offered. I felt like I belonged to a group of young ladies who genuinely cared for each other. I was probably one of the first ones at the meetings and the last to leave because it was my place of escape from the horrible things happening to me. If you ever feel alone, I would say get with a group of people who care about you and can uplift your spirits and empower you.

I realized that I was afraid to be alone and didn't really like myself, so I blamed myself for everything that happened to me over the years. We have to learn to love ourselves and stop asking or looking for people to validate us. "Is this outfit okay? How does my hair look? Do you think I should do this or do that?" We want to be the center of attention or we feel that people don't like us. We need to evaluate the people in our circle. If you keep surrounding yourself with yes people or people who always think you have the right answers to everything, you need to change your surroundings. You need some people who will keep it all the way real with you, who will tell you when you are wrong, even if it hurts. Sometimes we need that tough love to move us to the next level of thinking.

If you find yourself in an abusive situation, you need to have an escape plan. Have some clothes, money, and whatever you will need to start fresh in a safe place you can get to when you decide to leave.

If you have been isolated from family and friends, and don't know or have anywhere to go, call the National Domestic Violence Hotline at 1-800-799-SAFE (7233) or 1-800-787-3224 to get immediate assistance.

We must take our power back. Know that your pain has a purpose; our scars have a story; our mess has a message. Take the brokenness of the past and use it to give others a sense of hope and healing. I say these affirmations to encourage and *#SpeakLife* over myself:

I AM a virtuous woman.

I AM not weak, meek, or mild.

I AM a woman of power and a force to be reckoned with!

I recognize and celebrate me and my accomplishments.

My body is precious cargo, and it should be handled with care.

I AM living an abundant, purposeful life, and I will not allow the issues of my past to limit me.

I AM a leader, trustworthy, faithful, sympathetic, and compassionate to others.

I AM glad I have a personal and intimate relationship with GOD.

I rely on His strength and wisdom.

I AM strong, intelligent and beautiful—inside and out.

I AM loved, adored, and cherished.

I AM a willing vessel, ready to be used by God.

Lord, you are the potter and I am the clay. Mold me; have your way in my life!

Chandra

Bios

FACES OF DOMESTIC VIOLENCE SURVIVAL

• LA'TICIA NICOLE •

La'Ticia Nicole is a bestselling author, highly sought-after motivational speaker, philanthropist, mentor, and is always a work in progress. Her public speaking platform, *La'Ticia Nicole #SpeakLife*, has allowed her to motivate others by simply speaking life into the dead areas that cause people to feel broken and angry.

Her strong desire to empower, promote self-awareness and self-esteem throughout the communities at-large led her to create the nonprofit organization, Professional Divas, Inc. The term "entrepreneur" doesn't begin to describe who she is. She is a women of valor, a huge giver and an inspirational leader to many. To learn more, visit www.LaTiciaNicole.com.

• KIMBERLY SESSOMS •

Kimberly Sessoms was born and raised in Elizabeth City, NC on July 27, 1968 as the youngest of three children. A runner, businesswoman, motivator, prayer partner, encourager to many, and woman of God, she believes everyone has a purpose in life and wants to see everyone get all that God has intended for them to receive.

Kim earned her Associate's in General Office Technology at The College of the Albemarle in 1990, completed three years at CBI-Calvary Bible Institute in 1998 at Greater Mt. Calvary Holy Church in Washington, DC, and received her Bachelor's in Business Management from Kaplan University in 2009. As a member of the Professional Divas, she promotes events that bring awareness to underserved communities while raising funds for the cause.

She has two daughters, along with three grandsons, who she loves dearly. In addition to fulfilling her life's purpose, she loves spending time with her family and friends and knows that nothing is impossible with God.

• MARICE BEATTY •

Marice Beatty was born and raised in Winston-Salem, NC. She was once a teenage mother who many thought was going to be part of the statistics, not amounting to anything and living off the state for the rest of her life, but God had already designed a plan for her life. A single mother of two beautiful daughters, she obtained her BS in Nursing from WSSU in 1996 and began a career in the local hospitals. After a few years, Marice desired more in her profession and began a career in the travel nurse industry, where she met her loving husband, John, on her first assignment. They have been married for 14 years.

In 2007, Marice completed her dual master's degree, MS of Nursing and MBA in Health Care Management. In 2009, she established her own company, Traveling Professional CPR Consultant, after seeing the need for proactive education in the community. Her greatest goal in life is serving God with excellence in everything that she does.

• TAMICA JONES •

Tamica Alberta Jones was born in September of 1975 in Montgomery, Pennsylvania, the 18th child out of 20 children. She was raised in Winston-Salem, NC, where she received her formative education and attended Glenn High School. She later attained a Bachelor's in Social Work at Winston-Salem State University. In 2001, she joined the United States Army and served until 2008. Upon discharge from the military, she put her degree to work in the social work field.

Teaching and providing guidance to at-risk youth inspired her to pursue a Master's degree in Human Services at Coppin State University. Nothing has brought her more pleasure than the day God laid it on her heart to start Powerful Women of God (PWOG) to bring women of God together to encourage, inspire, network, teach, renew and restore. PWOG was birthed in 2010, and God has given it life since then. In 2012, along with her husband, Courtney Jones, started Noexcusezone, an apparel and healthy lifestyle brand.

• TRINITA L. WILLIAMS •

Trinita L. Williams is the founder of Professional Women Entrepreneurs, Inc., a nonprofit organization that provides guidance and support to women entrepreneurs and women who aspire to be entrepreneurs. It is her mission to provide education, motivation, and host events that will empower women to balance family, business and friends while not neglecting their ability to reach their highest potential. She has taken the lead in showing her fellow women entrepreneurs the essence of a true woman, which will always include heart, determination, support, enlightenment, honor and integrity. In 2012, she introduced her bath and body line, and makeup and skincare lines.

• KRISTIN MANGUM •

Kristen Mangum is a strong advocate that God makes no mistakes, so we must love ourselves as God loves us. Once a victim of domestic violence, she now speaks about her story from a place of power. She offers her emotional testimony on public platforms to encourage and empower other women to get to know God personally and intimately and to begin developing a relationship with themselves in spite of every flaw and blemish, inside and out.

At the age of 25, she earned her GED, then went on to the Hair Design School of Durham, where she earned the title of Adult Student Body President and her license in cosmetology. In addition to volunteering with Professional Divas, Inc., Kristen's passion is children. She has three children of her own—Serenity, O'marion and Syr'ajah—while also supporting her three godchildren—Keshaun, Kailee and Nevaeh—and serving young girls who cannot afford professional stylists.

• CHANDRA SOUTHERN •

Chandra P.A. Southern is a proud alumnus of Winston-Salem State University where she obtained a B.A. degree in Business Administration/Marketing in 1994. She currently holds a license in cosmetology and real estate in Georgia and North Carolina, as well as Certification in Nonprofit Organization Management. Furthermore, she's an authorized facilitator/educator of HIV/AIDS, Positive Youth Development and Character Development Leader, (CSEC)-Child Sexual Exploitation, and Stewardess of Children Child Sexual Abuse Awareness Curriculum. She is an active volunteer, a dedicated wife, mother, and mentor who enjoys spending time with family and friends.

Her passion is to be a beacon of light and make a difference in the lives of young people. As the founder and executive director of Delivered Vessels Inc., Chandra believes that if youth are given the tools, knowledge and empowerment to make positive decisions with their future, it will help mold our society. She also firmly stands on the belief that "God is able to do exceedingly and abundantly above all we can ask or think."

• SPICEE GRAY •

Spicee Gray is an author, motivational speaker and a strong, independent single mother who fought to overcome emotional scars of abuse at the hands of those she felt would love her for the woman she's become. Abuse to her is not just physical, but also verbal and mental, which traumatizes anyone and gives the same effect. Spicee escaped from thirteen years of marriage to her ex-husband and another seven years with her youngest one's dad. In both relationships, she experienced traumatizing abuse which kept her from knowing the true meaning of love.

The one day came where she finally allowed herself to break walls and open her heart towards both loving and being loved, but surprisingly she came to the fork in the road, resulting in her being in love all by herself once again. In her book of poetry, *The Unspoken Heart*, she aims her melodic truths at her past two relationships, friends, family, and the beloved woman reflected in the mirror. To learn more, visit www.about.me/SpiceeGray

Resources

DON'T SUFFER IN SILENCE,
GET THE HELP YOU NEED

1) **The National Domestic Violence Hotline**
   www.thehotline.org
   800-799-7233
   800-787-3224 (TTY)

2) **Family Violence Prevention Fund**
   www.endabuse.org
   415-252-8900
   800-595-4889 (TTY)

3) **National Coalition Against Domestic Violence**
   www.ncadv.org
   303-839-1852
   303-839-8459 (TTY)

4) **Safe Horizons**
   www.victimservices.org
   800-621-4673
   866-604-5350 (TTY)

5) **Battered Women's Justice Project**
   www.bwjp.org/bwjp_home
   800-903-0111, ext 1

6) **National Network to End Domestic Violence**
www.nnedv.org
800-799-7233
800-787-3224 (TTY)

7) **Rape, Abuse & Incest National Network**
www.rainn.org
800-656-HOPE

8) **Community United Against Violence**
www.cuav.org
415-777-5500

9) **FaithTrust Institute**
www.faithtrustinstitute.org
206-634-1903

10) **Futures Without Violence**
www.futureswithoutviolence.org
415-529-2930
800-595-4889 (TTY)

11) **INCITE!**
www.incite-national.org

Emergency Safety Plan

GET READY, BE PREPARED

VIOLENT INCIDENT

1. If I decide to leave, I will ______________________________. *(Practice how to get out safely. What doors, windows, elevators, stairwells or fire escapes would you use?)*

2. I can keep my purse and car keys ready and put them ______________________ (place) in order to leave quickly.

3. I can tell ____ about the violence and request they call the police if they hear suspicious noises coming from my house.

4. I can teach my children how to use the telephone to contact the police and the fire department.

5. I will use ____ as my code for my children or my friends so they can call for help.

6. If I have to leave my home, I will go _________________. *(Decide this even if you don't think there will be a next time).*

   If I cannot go to the location above, then I can go to

   ____

   or ____.

7. I can also teach some of these strategies to some/all of my children.

8. When I expect we are going to have an argument, I will try to move to a space that is lowest risk, such as ____.

   (Try to avoid arguments in the bathroom, garage, kitchen, near weapons or in rooms without access to an outside door).

PREPARING TO LEAVE

1. I will leave money and an extra set of keys with ______________________ so that I can leave quickly.

2. I will keep copies of important papers and documents or an extra set of keys at ______________________.

3. I will open a savings account by ______________, to increase my independence.

4. Other things I can do to increase my independence include:

   ____

   ____

   ____

5. The domestic violence program's hot line telephone number is ____________________ and I can seek shelter by calling this hot line.

6. I can keep change for phone calls on me at all times. I understand that if I use my telephone credit card, the following month the telephone bill will tell my batterer those numbers that I called after I left.

   To keep my telephone communications confidential, I must either use coins or I might get a friend to permit me to use their telephone credit card for a limited time when I first leave.

7. I will check with ______________________________ and ________________________ to see who would be able to let me stay with them or lend me some money in an emergency.

8. I can leave extra clothes with ____________________.

9. I will sit down and review my safety plan every ______ in order to plan the safest way to leave the residence.

10. ____________________________________ (domestic violence advocate or friend) has agreed to help me review this plan.

11. I will rehearse my escape plan and, as appropriate, practice it with my children.

IN MY OWN HOME

1. I can change the locks on my doors and windows as soon as possible.

2. I can replace wooden doors with steel/metal doors.

3. I can install security systems including additional locks, window bars, poles to wedge against doors, an electronic system, etc.

4. I can purchase rope ladders to be used for escape from second floor windows.

5. I can install smoke detectors and purchase fire extinguishers for each floor in my house/apartment.

6. I can install an outside lighting system that lights up when a person is coming close to my house.

7. I will teach my children how to use the telephone to make a collect call to me and to ______________________ (friend/minister/other) in the event that my partner takes the children.

8. I will tell people who take care of my children which people have permission to pick up my children and that my partner is not permitted to do so. The people I will inform about pick-up permission include:

   School ______________________________

   Daycare Staff ______________________________

Babysitter ____________________

Teacher ____________________

Pastor ____________________

Others ____________________

____

____

9. I can inform ____________________, and ____________________ (neighbors), ____________________ and, ____________________ (friend) that my partner no longer resides with me and they should call the police if he is observed near my residence.

SAFETY WITH AN ORDER OF PROTECTION

1. I will keep my protection order ______________________ (location). *(Always keep it on or near your person. If you change purses, that's the first thing that should go in)*

2. I will give my protection order to police departments in the communities where I usually visit family or friends, and in the community where I live.

3. The _____________ County Sheriff is the county registry of protection orders that all police departments can call to confirm a protection order. I can check to make sure that my order is in registry.

   The telephone number for the county registry of protection order is ____________________________.

4. I can call the local domestic violence program if I have questions or if I have some problem with my protection order.

5. I will inform my employer, my minister, my closest friend, my relatives, and ___________________________ and _____________________________________that I have a protection order in effect.

6. If my partner destroys my protection order, I can get another copy from the ________________________ County Courthouse by going to the Circuit Court Clerk's Office, or by contacting the Domestic Violence Unit of the ______________________________ County Prosecuting Attorney.

7. If my partner violates the protection order, I can call the police and report a violation, contact my attorney, call my advocate, and/or advise the court of the violation.

8. If the police do not help, I can contact my advocate or attorney and will file a complaint with the chief of the police department.

9. I can also file a private criminal compliant with the Prosecuting Attorney in the jurisdiction where the violation occurred.

   I can request that charges be filed against my battering partner for violation of the Protective Order and all the crimes that he commits in violating the order. I can call the domestic violence advocate for help.

ON THE JOB AND IN PUBLIC

1. I can inform my boss, the security supervisor and ______________________________ at work of my situation.

2. I can ask ____________________________________ to help screen my telephone calls at work.

3. When leaving work, I can ________________________.

4. When driving home if problems occur, I can ________.

5. If I use public transit, I can _______________________.

6. I will go to different grocery stores and shopping malls to conduct my business and shop at hours that are different than those when residing with my battered partner.

7. I can use a different bank and take care of my banking at hours different from those I used when residing with my battered partner.

8. I can also____________________________________.

WHEN I LEAVE, I SHOULD HAVE:

1. Identification for myself
2. Children's birth certificate
3. My birth certificate
4. Social security cards
5. School and vaccination records
6. Money
7. Checkbook, ATM card, Credit cards
8. Keys: house, car and/or office
9. Driver's license and registration
10. Medication
11. Welfare identification, work permits, Green Card,
12. Passport, divorce papers
13. Medical records - for all family members
14. Lease/rental agreement, house deed, mortgage book
15. Bank books, Insurance papers
16. Small saleable objects
17. Address book, pictures, jewelry
18. Children's favorite toys and/or blankets
19. Items of special sentimental value

TELEPHONE NUMBERS I NEED TO KNOW:

Emergency 911

State Police ____________________

County Police ____________________

County Sheriff ____________________

Work number ____________________

Supervisor's number ____________________

Pastor ____________________

Other ____________________

County Prosecuting Attorney Domestic Violence Unit

____

County Registry of Protection Orders County Sheriff

____

I will keep this document in a safe place and out of the reach of my potential attacker.

WE WANT TO HEAR FROM YOU!!!

If this book has made a difference in your life or in the life of someone you know, La'Ticia would be delighted to hear about it. **Leave a review on Amazon.com!**

Book La'Ticia to speak at your event!

Send an email to admin@laticianicole.com
or visit her website:

www.LaTiciaNicole.com

• • •

Follow La'Ticia on social media

"EMPOWERING YOU TO IMPACT GENERATIONS"
www.PublishYourGift.com

www.ingramcontent.com/pod-product-compliance
Lightning Source LLC
Chambersburg PA
CBHW070447170726
48291CB00005B/1635

* 9 7 8 1 9 4 2 8 3 8 1 7 3 *